SINGER'S LIBRARY OF ARIAS

15 VOCAL MASTERWORKS FROM THE BAROQUE ERA THROUGH THE TWENTY-FIRST CENTURY

COMPILED, EDITED AND ARRANGED BY PATRICK M. LIEBERGEN

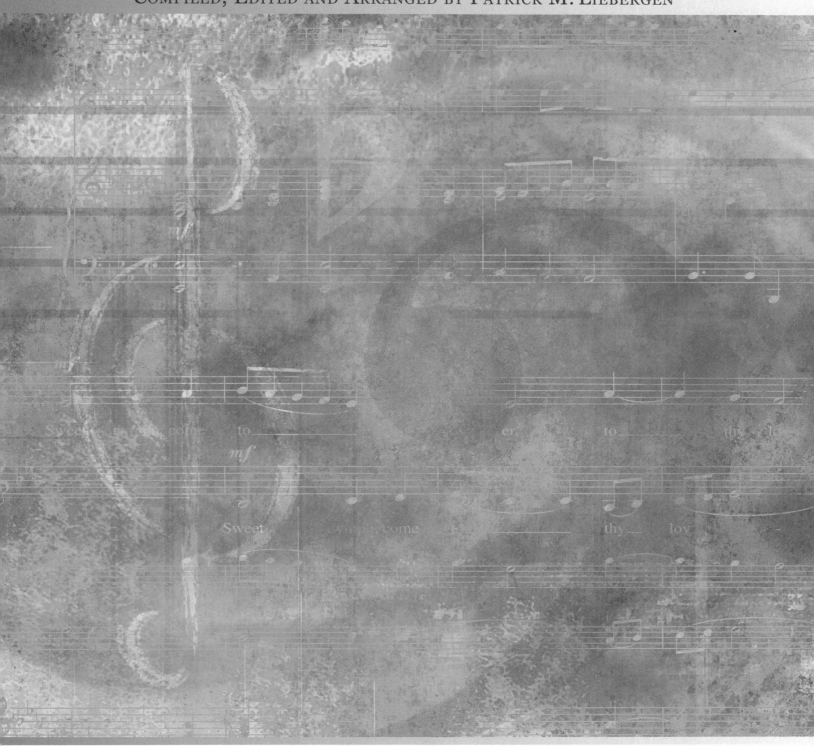

Medium Low Book (28814)
ISBN-10: 0-7390-5140-7
ISBN-13: 978-0-7390-5140-5
Medium Low Book & CD (28816)
ISBN-10: 0-7390-5142-3
ISBN-13: 978-0-7390-5142-9
Medium Low Accompaniment CD (28815)
ISBN-10: 0-7390-5141-5
ISBN-13: 978-0-7390-5141-2

Medium High Book (28811)
ISBN-10: 0-7390-5137-7
ISBN-13: 978-0-7390-5137-5
Medium High Book & CD (28813)
ISBN-10: 0-7390-5139-3
ISBN-13: 978-0-7390-5139-9
Medium High Accompaniment CD (28812)
ISBN-10: 0-7390-5138-5
ISBN-13: 978-0-7390-5138-2

Contents

Foreword

Singer's Library of Arias features fifteen of the world's best-loved selections brought together for the first time in one collection. Representing a wide range of styles and composers, these vocal solos from the Baroque era through the twenty-first century are presented with historical information and suggestions for performance. Additionally, pronunciation guides and translations are included for all arias with foreign texts. Selected, edited and arranged by Patrick M. Liebergen, this truly valuable collection is an indispensable resource for the singer.

The preparation of this anthology involved a number of editorial considerations. Original scores were consulted in the preparation of the editions when possible, and any changes are noted in the editor's comments for each selection. If instrumental accompaniments were included in the original scores, then the keyboard accompaniments in this edition are reductions of those parts. Separate instrumental parts are included in the back of this book for the performance of "*Domine Deus*," "Sheep May Safely Graze" and "You Raise Me Up."

An IPA Pronunciation Guide is provided on page 119 of this book for reference in using the pronunciation guides. While the pronunciation guides are a helpful resource, they cannot replace the experience and expertise of a professional vocal coach or music teacher.

Singer's Library of Arias is available in Medium High and Medium Low voicings, with or without compact disc recordings of the accompaniments. These accompaniments, masterfully recorded by Sally K. Albrecht, may be useful for both rehearsal and performance.

Acknowledgements

I would like to thank Sally K. Albrecht, Andy Beck and Martha T. Buchta, my editors at Alfred Publishing Company, for their wisdom and excellent suggestions in the preparation of this anthology.

Patrick M. Liebergen
April, 2008

Patrick M. Liebergen

Patrick M. Liebergen is widely published as a choral editor, arranger and composer of masterwork vocal and choral editions, collections and cantatas, as well as original choral works. The Director of Choral Activities at the University of Wisconsin-Stout in Menomonie, Wisconsin, Dr. Liebergen has served in a variety of positions as a leader of school and church music. With music degrees from St. Norbert College in DePere, WI, the University of Wisconsin-Madison and the University of Colorado-Boulder, he frequently appears throughout the country as a conductor and clinician. Dr. Liebergen has received choral composition awards from the Twin Cities Church Musicians' Association, the Wisconsin Choral Directors' Association and ASCAP, and his works have been performed around the world.

Sally K. Albrecht

The piano performances on the Accompaniment CDs are by Sally K. Albrecht. Sally is the Director of School Choral Publications for Alfred Publishing. She is a popular choral conductor, composer and clinician, and has degrees in Music and Theatre from Rollins College and an M.A. in Drama and an M.M. in Accompanying from the University of Miami.

Domine Deus
(Lord, God Forever)

Antonio Vivaldi (1678–1741)

Antonio Vivaldi was a renowned composer and violin virtuoso in Venice, Italy, during the Baroque era. Born into a family of musicians, he studied composition and violin with his father, a violinist at St. Mark's in Venice, and later with Giovanni Legrenzi. Ordained a Roman Catholic priest in 1703, he eventually ended his career as an active priest in the church due to ill health and problems with the church authorities concerning his behavior as a priest. Vivaldi spent most of his life after 1709 teaching orphaned girls at the Conservatory of the Pieta in Venice while conducting, composing, performing and teaching music. As choirmaster at this school for homeless girls, he composed numerous instrumental and choral works for the performances of the students, often conducting Saturday and Sunday evening concerts of his music. Called the "prete rosse" (red priest) because of his hair, his fame soon spread for his musical talents as a composer and violinist.

Vivaldi is especially known today for his instrumental works, which include over five hundred concertos. His set of four violin concertos known as the *The Four Seasons (Le quattro Stagioni)* is his best-known work and is among the most popular pieces of Baroque music today. He also wrote sonatas, chamber works, operas and a variety of sacred choral works, of which his *Gloria* RV 589 is best known and most performed. Vivaldi's style is characterized by driving rhythm, clarity and lyrical melody. He helped standardize the three-movement concerto form later used by other Baroque composers, such as Johann Sebastian Bach, and he was one of the most significant figures in the transition from late Baroque to early classical style.

"*Domine Deus*" is the sixth movement of Vivaldi's *Gloria*, which was composed for performance at the Pieta. Vivaldi actually completed another *Gloria* RV 588 in the same key and around the same period with similar scoring. But the best known version has remained one of the cornerstones of Baroque repertoire.

Vivaldi set "*Domine Deus*" as a duet between a soprano soloist and an oboe or violin over continuo. It is a siciliano, a Baroque form in 6/8 or 12/8 meter, which is usually characterized with lilting rhythms in a pastoral dance. A siciliano in the eighteenth-century was associated with shepherds and idyllic country life, often projecting the image of the Good Shepherd. The original Latin words of "*Domine Deus*" depict God not only as the King of Heaven but also as a tender and loving Father.

This edition appears here in the original key. The keyboard part features a realization of Vivaldi's continuo part in addition to the violin or oboe solo in the event that a solo instrument is not available. Optional English words and dynamic indications have also been added. The original instrumental parts can be found on pages 112–114.

"*Domine Deus*" should be performed quite smoothly with a constant beat while the singer gives a slight emphasis to the naturally energized syllables.

PRONUNCIATION GUIDE

Do-mi-ne De-us, Rex coe-le-stis,
dɔ-mi-nɛ dɛ-us, rɛks chɛ-lɛ-stis,

De-us Pa-ter o-mni-po-tens.
dɛ-us pɑ-tɛr ɔ-mni-pɔ-tɛns.

Footnotes to Latin Pronunciation

- In multiple syllable words, the syllables that should be stressed are underlined.

- [r] should be rolled.

- [ɾ] should be flipped.

TRANSLATION

Lord, God, Heavenly King,
God the Father almighty.

1. Domine Deus

(Lord, God Forever)

with optional violin or oboe solo and cello*

English words by
PATRICK M. LIEBERGEN

from GLORIA
Music by
ANTONIO VIVALDI (1678-1741)
Edited by **PATRICK M. LIEBERGEN**

*Optional Violin or Oboe part is on page 112. Optional Cello part is on pages 113–114.

Gioite al canto mio

(Rejoice, O Hear My Singing)

Jacopo Peri (1561–1633)

Jacopo Peri was a very significant Florentine composer of his time, completing a number of musical dramas with innovations that greatly influenced other late Renaissance and early Baroque composers. Also a singer and instrumentalist, Peri is important today for having composed *Dafne*, the first dramatic work featuring continuous music. He wrote it with the collaboration of his patron Jacopo Corsi and the poet Ottavio Rinuccini. First performed in 1598, it was among the first of its kind to be written in monodic style, which consisted of vocal solos clearly declaiming the Italian words with the support of a few instruments. This work was probably written as a result of his meeting with a group of other Renaissance poets and musicians, called the "Camerata," who were eager to revive the declamation of Greek drama. The efforts of these artists, including Giovanni de' Bardi, Giulio Caccini and Jacopo Corsi, resulted in the development of recitative and a number of music dramas. Since most of the music of *Dafne* is lost, Peri's *Euridice*, his second collaboration with Rinuccini, is important, for the printings of this opera exist today. Completed and performed in 1600 to celebrate the marriage of Maria de' Medici and Henry IV of France, the original copies of this opera are the first published examples available of Peri's settings of narrations and dialogues for solo voices with continuo accompaniment in a dramatic format. These scores reveal that Peri's continuo part, moving slower than that of Caccini's, allows for a more parlando style of declamation by the voice.

The story of the libretto is based on the Greek myth that Orpheus, through the power of his singing, is able to gain entrance to the underworld to rescue his bride, Euridice, who had died of a snake bite. "*Gioite al canto mio*" is sung by Orpheus in the fifth and final section of this one-movement opera, when he finally returns with Euridice to the living world.

The sweeping phrases of this very joyous aria should be sung by greatly sustaining the vowels while energizing the naturally accented syllables. It was Peri's intention that the word inflections closely coincide with the rhythms of the music, and that the emotion of the words be especially heard in this new expressive style. To enhance the declamation of the text in *Euridice*, Peri did away with the Renaissance practice of independent lines, including only a singular bass part and a few indications for chordal harmonies to be sounded by a small number of instrumentalists, such as violins, recorders, harpsichord and lute. There is also evidence in his preface to *Euridice* that instruments such as the harpsichord, lira da gamba, bass lute and chitarrone played behind the scenes at the first performance. In accordance with additional descriptions of early seventeenth century performances, it would be acceptable for "*Gioite al canto mio*" to be accompanied by the additional use of strings and melodic wind instruments (recorders or flutes) to enhance the sound with a discreet and simple accompaniment.

The source for this edition is the publication of Giorgio Marescotti, printed in 1600 in Florence, Italy. The note values of the original white mensural notation have been halved. The key in Marescotti's version has been retained for this edition. Modern clefs, dynamic and tempo indications and optional English words have been included by the editor.

PRONUNCIATION GUIDE

Gio-i-te al can-to mi-o, sel-ve fron-do-se,
dʒɔ-i-tɛal kan-tɔ mi-ɔ, sɛl-vɛ frɔn-do-zɛ,

Gio-i-te a-ma-ti col-li, e-d'o-gn'in-tor-no,
dʒɔ-i-tɛa-ma-ti kɔlːli ɛ-do-ɲin-tor-nɔ,

Ec-co rim-bom-bi dal-le val-li a-sco-se.
ɛ-kɔ rim-bom-bi dalːlɛ valːlia-sko-zɛ.

Ri-sor-to è'l mio bel sol di rag-gi a-dor-no,
ri-sor-tɔɛl miɔ bɛl sol di radːdʒia-dor-nɔ,

E co' be-gl'oc-chi, on-de fa scor-no a De-lo,
e kɔ bɛ-ʎɔkːki, on-dɛ fa skɔr-nɑa dɛ-lɔ,

Rad-dop-pia fo-co a l'al-me, e lu-ce al gior-no,
radːdopːpja fɔ-kɔalːlal-me lu-tʃɛal dʒor-nɔ,

E fa ser-vi d'a-mor la ter-ra e'l Cie-lo.
e fa sɛr-vi da-mor la tɛrːrael tʃɛ-lɔ.

Footnotes to Italian Pronunciation

- In multiple syllable words, the syllables that should be stressed are underlined.
- [ɲ] indicates that the tip of the tongue should be in contact with the lower front teeth while the front of the tongue is raised and pressed against the front of the hard palate. Nasality is then produced when breath passes through the nose.
- [r] should be trilled.
- [ʎ] indicates a similar sound to [lj] in the word "begl'occhi" [bɛ-ʎɔkːki].
- Certain double consonants can be sustained on a pitch while maintaining a legato line, such as those in the words "colli" and "valli." The singer should take time for the singable double consonants in each of these words from the preceding musical note.
- There are other double consonants, such as those in the words "raggi" and "occhi," which interrupt the legato line when pronounced correctly. For example, when singing the word "raggi" [radːdʒi], the singer should briefly stop on the [d], creating a slight silence before the sounding of the [dʒ].

TRANSLATION

Rejoice at my song, leafy woods,
Rejoice, beloved hills and from all around
May the echo resound from the hidden valleys.
Resurrected is my beautiful sun adored with rays,
And with beautiful eyes, which makes scorn to Delos,
She redoubles fire to souls and light to the day,
And makes Heaven and earth the servants of love.

2. Gioite al canto mio

(Rejoice, O Hear My Singing)

Italian words by
OTTAVIO RINUCCINI (1562-1612)
English words by **PATRICK M. LIEBERGEN**

from EURIDICE
Music by **JACOPO PERI** (1561-1633)
Arranged by **PATRICK M. LIEBERGEN**

I Attempt from Love's Sickness

Henry Purcell (1659–1695)

Beloved by the English people and recognized as a genius in his own lifetime, Henry Purcell was a highly talented Baroque composer and one of the greatest English composers of all time. Beginning his musical experiences as a chorister in the Chapel Royal, Purcell had quite a varied and successful career. He was appointed composer to the King in 1677 and the organist of Westminster Abbey in 1679. He served in his church music position until his death, providing music for the coronation of two English kings and for the funeral of Queen Mary. He also contributed to the 1694 edition of Playford's instruction book titled *An Introduction to the Skill of Musick* and wrote music for theatrical productions in the latter portion of his life.

His greatness can be seen in the large number and variety of works of the highest quality which he wrote during his short life of only 36 years. Besides many odes and welcome songs for chorus and orchestra, cantatas, songs, catches, anthems, services, fancies, chamber sonatas, keyboard works and a variety of other instrumental pieces, he wrote several semi-operas and incidental music for numerous plays. His *Dido and Aeneas* was the first great English opera.

Beginning in 1690 until his death, Purcell became quite involved in writing for the operatic market, for success in the theatre gave him a much higher income than the occasional performances of his odes, welcome songs and anthems.

Completing his semi-operas and providing incidental music for plays resulted in increased sales of his music in print.

"I Attempt from Love's Sickness" is a lively song from the semi-opera *The Indian Queen* z 630, Purcell's largest stage project in 1695. For his last music drama, Purcell chose an improbable story, from a play with the same name, which was the collaboration of John Dryden and his brother-in-law, Sir Robert Howard. The plot involves a theme of war between Peru and Mexico and also love relationships between individuals in the Inca and Aztec empires. Set in six acts, it is in the third act that the Spirits of the Air encourage Zempoalla, queen of the Mexicans, to forget her love for the Peruvian General, Montezuma. Zempoalla acknowledges her incapacity to escape with the singing of "I Attempt from Love's Sickness."

Originally scored for high voice and continuo only, this edition is in the original key and includes the addition of the four measure introduction and a keyboard accompaniment adapted from the original continuo part. Modern clefs and tempo and dynamic indications have also been added.

Although "I Attempt from Love's Sickness" is performed by a soprano in a performance of *The Indian Queen*, this solo is an excellent choice for singers of other voice classifications, for it enables singers to work on vocal technique and to experience the style of a truly gifted composer of Baroque music.

3. I Attempt from Love's Sickness

Words by **ROBERT HOWARD** (1626–1698)
and **JOHN DRYDEN** (1631–1700)

from THE INDIAN QUEEN
Music by **HENRY PURCELL** (1659–1695)
Edited by **PATRICK M. LIEBERGEN**

sick - ness to fly_____ in vain, Since

I am my - self my own fe - ver, since I am my -

self my own fe - ver_____ and_____ pain. For love has more_____

pow'r and less mer - cy than fate, To make us_____ seek_____

I Got Plenty O' Nuttin'

George Gershwin (1898–1937)

The American composer, pianist and conductor George Gershwin wrote works for both Broadway and the classical concert hall. Also successful at composing popular songs, most of his vocal and theatrical works were in collaboration with his elder brother, lyricist Ira Gershwin.

Born in Brooklyn, New York, George Gershwin became a highly skilled pianist at a young age. After studying piano in the European classical tradition, he began his career selling songs, singing and playing them at the piano for a publishing company in Tin Pan Alley. Achieving his first big national hit with his song "Swanee," he continued to compose popular songs, many of which were featured in his more than a dozen Broadway shows. Standards such as "Fascinating Rhythm," "Embraceable You," "Someone to Watch Over Me," "I Got Rhythm" and "Oh, Lady Be Good!" have been regularly performed by leading vocal artists to this day. Gershwin's very successful musicals included *Strike up the Band*, *Girl Crazy* and *Of Thee I Sing*, which won a Pulitzer Prize for drama.

Gershwin continued classical training while exploring jazz elements in his formative years, achieving much success throughout his brief career. His first major classical work, *Rhapsody in Blue* for orchestra and piano, proved to be his most popular work, drawing rave reviews for his ability to unite jazz elements with the classical style. Especially influenced by French composers and music of other international composers, his *Concerto in F* and *An American in Paris* reflects his interest to learn and change as a composer. He made his debut as a conductor when he conducted the New York Philharmonic Orchestra at Lewisohn Stadium in New York in a performance of *An American in Paris* and *Rhapsody in Blue*, playing the piano part of the latter himself. It was Gershwin's tremendous ability at combining European orchestral techniques with American jazz and folk music idioms that contributed to the creation of his most ambitious work, *Porgy and Bess*.

Porgy and Bess is widely regarded as the most important American opera of our time. The libretto by Du Bose Heyward was based on his own play *Porgy*, which opened on Broadway in 1927, eight years before the opera *Porgy and Bess*. Gershwin had read Heyward's book *Porgy* when it became a bestseller in 1926, thereafter deciding to compose a full-length opera based on Heyward's story about life among the black inhabitants of 'Catfish Row' in Charleston, South Carolina. After the Gershwin brothers and Heyward signed a contract in 1933, Gershwin began the score in 1934. Billed as "An American folk opera" and with lyrics by Ira Gershwin and Dorothy Heyward, the opera *Porgy and Bess* premiered in a Broadway theatre in 1935 with an entire cast of classically trained African-American singers. George Gershwin successfully incorporated a wealth of blues and jazz idioms into the classical art form of opera, creating an operatic standard for both national and international performance. His roots in jazz, drawing on southern black traditions, is evident in this opera. Each selection was modeled after a type of black folk song, such as the blues, praying song, work song and spiritual, all of which were blended with the traditional operatic style.

The story of *Porgy and Bess* involves the main character, Porgy, a crippled black man living in the slums of Charleston, South Carolina, and his attempts to rescue Bess from the clutches of Crown, her pimp, and Sportin' Life, the drug dealer. "I Got Plenty O' Nuttin'" sung by Porgy at the beginning of Act II, is just one of many songs that have been extracted from the original operatic setting for use in jazz and blues performance today. Some of the more popular pieces from the opera include "Summertime," "A Woman Is A Sometime Thing," "Bess, You Is My Woman Now," "It Ain't Necessarily So," "I Loves You, Porgy" and "O Lawd, I'm On My Way."

"I Got Plenty O' Nuttin'" is a musical break from the troubles of Porgy when he happily states his outlook on life. Porgy proclaims with a great smile that he has nothing but his gal, his Lord and his song, for that is all that he needs in life. The original orchestration calls for a banjo lightly sounding the vamp-like chords against the tuneful and exuberant melody of the soloist. The keyboard part should therefore be played very lightly in the manner of plucking banjo strings while emphasizing the two main pulsations in each measure. The original published version of 1935 features an eleven measure interlude of choral singing between the two verses of the soloist, all of which is deleted in this arrangement in order to merely provide the solo part. The original words found in the 1935 published score are included here. Sung by a bass-baritone in the original 1935 performance, this arrangement has been transposed up a minor third from the original key of G major for a medium-high male voice.

4. I Got Plenty O' Nuttin'

from PORGY AND BESS ®
Music and Lyrics by **GEORGE GERSHWIN** (1898-1937),
DU BOSE (1885-1940) and **DOROTHY HEYWARD** (1890-1961)
and **IRA GERSHWIN** (1896-1983)
Arranged by **PATRICK M. LIEBERGEN**

door,   (dat's no way to   be). _____   Dey kin steal de

rug   from de floor, _____   dat's o - keh wid   me,   'cause de things   dat I

prize,   like de stars   in de skies,   all are free. _____   Oh,

I   got   plen - ty o'   nut - tin', _____   an'   nut - tin's   plen - ty   fo'

La donna è mobile

(Woman Is Changeable)

Giuseppe Verdi (1813–1901)

"*La donna è mobile*" is one of the most easily remembered and immediately infectious opera tunes ever written. It is an essential part of the plot of Giuseppe Verdi's beloved masterpiece *Rigoletto*, a staple of the standard operatic repertoire.

The Italian nationalist composer Giuseppe Verdi is best known for his twenty-eight operas, for they exemplify the spirit of Romantic drama and passion. Born poor in a small town in northern Italy, Verdi faced a number of crises in his life, with the death of two of his children and his first wife, before achieving great success as a composer. When the director of *La Scala* insisted that Verdi return to composing after his string of tragedies, the result was the opera *Nabucco*, a triumph for the twenty-nine-year-old composer and the beginning of his spectacular career. Although he became famous around the world, Verdi maintained his simplicity while continuing to write incredibly memorable melodies for the common people. After producing one masterpiece after another, his final opera *Falstaff* was completed when he was eighty years old. When he died at the age of eighty-seven, Italy gave him the rites normally accorded a national hero. His funeral procession was graced with thousands of people joining as one in singing the memorable "*Va pensiero*" melody from his opera *Nabucco*.

Composed in 1851, *Rigoletto* was adapted from a 1832 melodrama titled *Le Roi s'Amuse (The King is Amused)* by the French playwright Victor Hugo. The production of that play in Paris in 1832 had provoked a scandal because the plot involved a frivolous king, supposedly Francois I of France, being victimized by his hunchbacked jester. Nevertheless, Verdi was very interested in the highly controversial subject for its dramatic possibilities on stage, and ultimately enlisted Francesco Maria Piave to translate it into an effective libretto for his upcoming opera. With libretto in hand, Verdi progressed well with the music in preparation for it's first performance in Venice to inaugurate the new *Teatro La Fenice* until the censor in Venice sent Verdi a letter informing him that the opera had to be cancelled because of the theme. Only after Verdi agreed to change the locale and the names of the characters, with the King of France becoming an imaginary Duke of Mantua, the opera was allowed to be performed.

Presented for the first time in 1851, the opera was an enormous and immediate success, especially the Duke's performance of "*La donna è mobile*." Verdi had not even shown that aria to the tenor until two days before the first performance, because it was so singable, and Verdi did not want it sung by the gondoliers in Venice before it was sung in the theater. It has since become one of the most popular operatic arias of all time.

It is an important and memorable moment in *Rigoletto* when the Duke of Mantua enters an inn disguised as a soldier to sing "*La donna è mobile*." He not only conveys his view of women, for the Duke also makes his philosophy of life clear. The aria is a brilliant summary of his frivolous and cynical character. "*La donna è mobile*" is an expression of his whole personality, and he sings it to amuse himself.

This energetic song is accompanied by a guitar-like orchestral strumming in the original version. After the orchestra first sounds the famous melody, it is heard numerous times in a strophic setting that brings back the opening text as a refrain. Verdi's original orchestration of woodwinds, brass and strings has been reduced to a keyboard accompaniment in this arrangement. The articulations and tempo markings included here are found in the original version. Verdi's dynamic indications have been slightly modified in this arrangement for performance by voice and piano alone, and optional English words and the optional cadenza traditionally performed by many opera stars today have also been included by the editor. This edition appears in its original key.

Often sung by leading tenors around the world, this aria should be energetically and rhythmically performed with a continuous pulse on the first beat of each measure. The singer should carefully follow Verdi's original articulations while emphasizing the naturally energized syllables of the Italian words and closely following the dynamic changes in order to contrast the various phrases.

PRONUNCIATION GUIDE

La don-na̲ è mo-bi-le qual piu-ma̲ al ven-to,
la ḏon:naɛ m̲ɔ-bi-lɛ kwal piu-mal v̲ɛn-tɔ,

mu-ta d'ac-cen-to e di pen-sie-ro.
m̲u-ta dat:tʃɛn-tɔ e di pɛn-sj̲ɛ-rɔ.

Sem-pre un̲ a-ma-bi-le leg-gia-dro vi-so,
s̲ɛm-prɛ una-m̲a-bi-lɛ led:dʒa-drɔ v̲i-zɔ,

in pian-to̲ o̲ in ri-so, è men-zo-gne-ro.
in pjan-tɔin r̲i-sɔ, ɛ men-tso-ɲ̲ɛ-rɔ.

La don-na̲ è mo-bil qual piu-ma̲ al ven-to,
la ḏon:naɛ m̲ɔ-bil kwal p̲iu-mal v̲ɛn-tɔ,

mu-ta d'ac-cen-to e di pen-sier.
m̲u-ta dat:tʃɛn-tɔ e di pɛn-sj̲ɛr.

È sem-pre mi-se-ro chi̲ a lei s'af-fi-da,
ɛ s̲ɛm-prɛ m̲i-ze-rɔ kja lɛi sa-f̲i-da,

chi le con-fi-da mal cau-to̲ il co-re!
k̲i lɛ kon-f̲i-da mal c̲au-tɔil k̲ɔ-rɛ!

Pur mai non sen-te-si fe-li-ce̲ ap-pie-no
pur mai nɔn s̲ɛn-te-zi fe-l̲i-tʃɛap-pj̲ɛ-nɔ

chi su quel se-no no li-ba̲ a-mo-re!
k̲i su kwel s̲e-nɔ non l̲i-ba-m̲o-rɛ!

La don-na̲ è mo-bil qual piu-ma̲ al ven-to,
la ḏon:naɛ m̲ɔ-bil kwal p̲iu-mal v̲ɛn-tɔ,

mu-ta d'ac-cen-to e di pen-sier.
m̲u-ta dat:tʃɛn-tɔ e di pɛn-sj̲ɛr.

Footnotes to Italian Pronunciation

- In multiple syllable words, the syllables that should be stressed are underlined.

- [ɲ] indicates that the tip of the tongue should be in contact with the lower front teeth while the front of the tongue is raised and pressed against the front of the hard palate. Nasality is then produced when breath passes through the nose.

- [ɾ] should be flipped.

- [r] should be trilled.

- Certain double consonants can be sustained on a pitch while maintaining a legato line, such as those in the word "donna." The singer should take time for the singable double consonants in each of these words from the preceding musical note.

- There are other double consonants, such as those in the words "accento" and "leggiadro," which interrupt the legato line when pronounced correctly. For example, when singing the word "accento" [at:tʃɛn-tɔ], the singer should briefly stop on the [t], creating a slight silence before the sounding of the [tʃ].

TRANSLATION

Woman is fickle, like a feather in the wind,
she changes her tone and her thoughts.
Always with a lovely face,
in tears or in laughter, she is lying.

He is always miserable, who trusts her,
who confides in her, his heart without caution!
Yet he never feels completely happy,
who upon that breast does not taste love!

5. La donna è mobile

(Woman Is Changeable)

Italian words by
FRANCESO MARIA PIAVE (1810–1876)
English words by **PATRICK M. LIEBERGEN**

from RIGOLLETO
Music by **GIUSEPPE VERDI** (1813–1901)
Edited and Arranged by **PATRICK M. LIEBERGEN**

La don - na è mo - bi - le
Wom - an is change - a - ble,

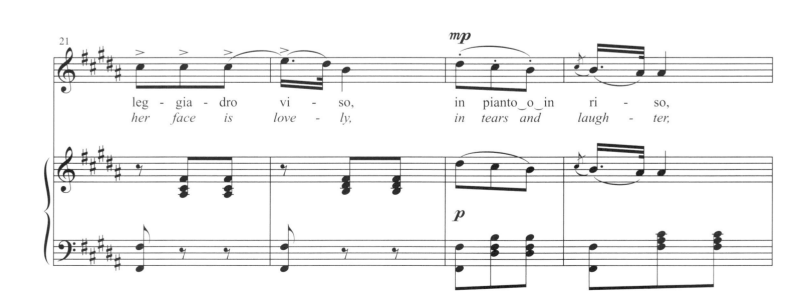

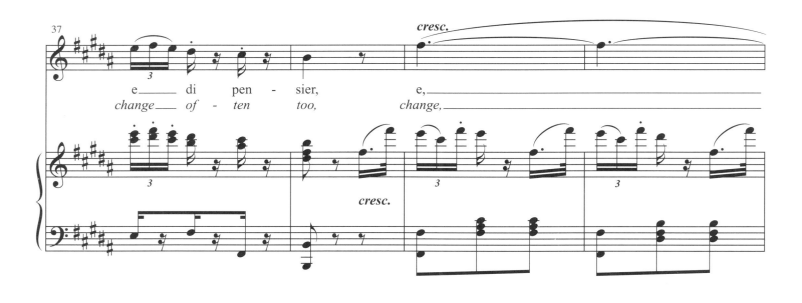

È sem - pre mi - se - ro
He'll al - ways feel____ pain,
chi a lei s'af -
that's if he

fi - da,
trusts____ her,
chi le con - fi - da
con - fid - ing to____ her,
mal cau - to il
not think - ing

co - re! / Pur mai non sen - te - si / fe - li - ce_ap -
clear - ly! / *Yet he will nev - er be* / *hap - py, con -*

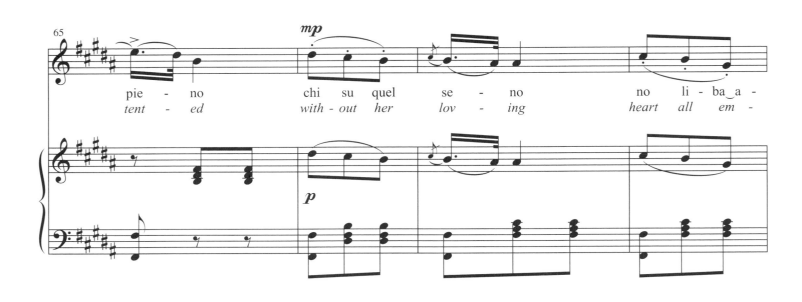

pie - no / chi su quel se - no / no li - ba_a -
tent - ed / *with - out her lov - ing* / *heart all em -*

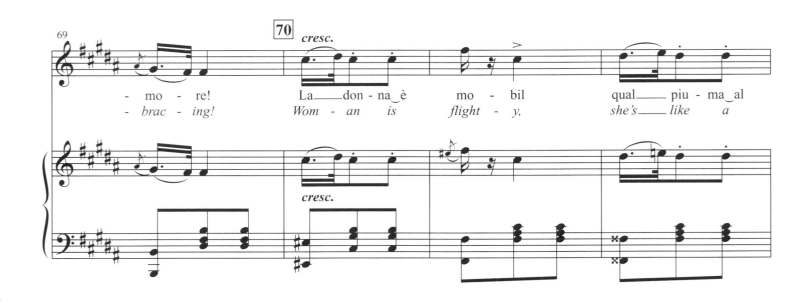

- mo - re! / La___ don - na_è mo - bil / qual___ piu - ma_al
- brac - ing! / *Wom - an is flight - y,* / *she's___ like a*

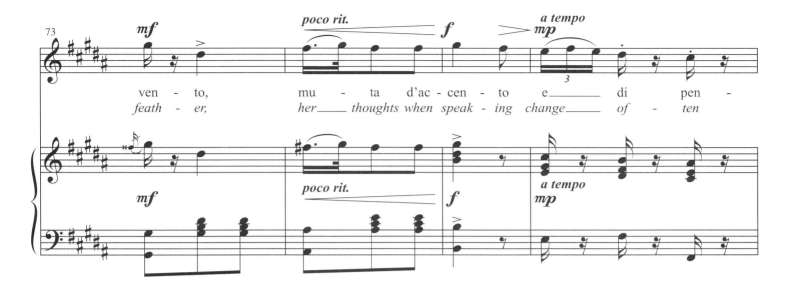

ven - to, mu - ta d'ac - cen - to e___ di pen -
feath - er, her___ thoughts when speak - ing change___ of - ten

sier, e___ di pen -
too, change___ of - ten

sier, e,___
too, change,___

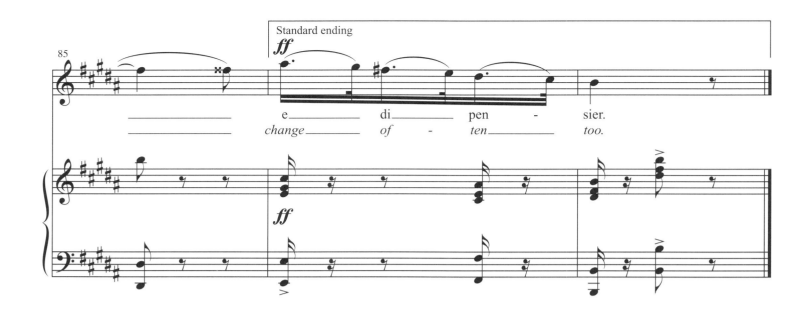

Standard ending

e _____ di _____ pen - sier.

change _____ of - ten _____ too.

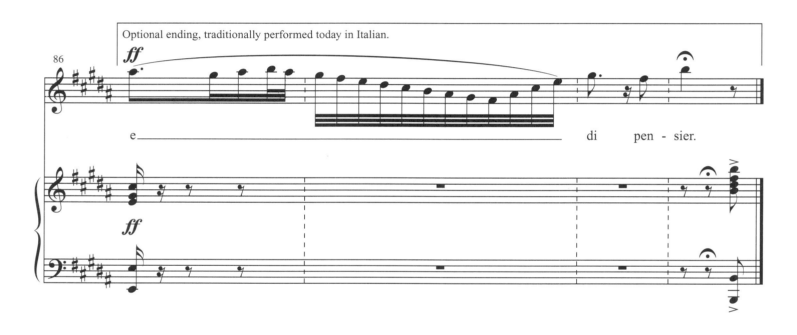

Optional ending, traditionally performed today in Italian.

e _____ di pen - sier.

Non siate ritrosi
(Oh, Don't You Be Shy)

Wolfgang Amadeus Mozart (1756–1791)

Mozart was one of the greatest musical geniuses of all time, and his work is exemplary of the Viennese classical style. He excelled in composing all the forms of his time, including operas, symphonies, concertos, chamber works, sonatas, choral works, arias and songs. A prolific and influential composer with over 600 compositions, his works are highly revered today for their beautiful melodies and rich harmonies.

Born in Salzburg, Austria, to a very musical family, Mozart's genius was apparent at a very early age. Concert tours with his father made Mozart a well-known performer in many European cities by his early teens. At the age of fourteen, he became concertmaster for the Archbishop of Salzburg. Although he was given the opportunity to compose in a great number of genres, he grew discontented with his low salary and the lack of opportunity for more opera composition in Salzburg. In 1781, against his father's advice, Mozart quit the position in Salzburg and settled in Vienna.

His early years in Vienna were met with many successes. He became known as the finest keyboard player in the city, and he completed a variety of works, including piano concertos and operas, that fully established his reputation as a composer. Despite becoming famous from his public concerts, Mozart's career and finances gradually declined. He spent his remaining years struggling for recognition and commissions without the security of a permanent position.

Mozart's style was characterized by clarity and balance. Over the course of his career, he switched his interests from instrumental music to operas and then back to instrumental composition. His operatic output included the styles of his time in Europe: opera seria, such as *Idomeneo*, Singspiel, of which *Die Zauberflöte* is an excellent example, and opera buffa, including *Le nozze di Figaro* and *Così fan tutte*. The title of the latter is often shortened to merely *Così* today.

Composed in 1789, *Così fan tutte* was first performed in 1790. It was the last of his three Italian comedies to librettos by Lorenzo da Ponte and the last work that he wrote for Emperor Joseph II's court opera company in Vienna. Unlike its predecessors *Le nozze di Figaro* K 492 and *Don Giovanni* K 527, which are based on pre-existing plays, the origins of *Così fan tutte* are not clearly documented. The main plot of the opera concerns a wager that two officers, Ferrando and Guglielmo, make with an old nobleman named Don Alfonso. The nobleman bets that the officers' fiancées, Dorabella and Fiodiligi, will not remain faithful to them, and he subsequently calls for having the officers disguise themselves to woo each others' fiancée. Although both Dorabella and Fiorgiligi agree to marry the supposed lovers and Alfonso wins his wager, he counsels the officers to take their fiancées back because after all, "*così fan tutte*"—"all women are like that."

"*Non siate ritrosi*" is sung by Guglielmo in the first act when he appears in disguise as an Albanian with Ferrando in an attempt to win over the sisters Dorabella and Fiodiligi. Guglielmo describes their many virtues, including their big muscles and their large mustaches.

The source of this edition is *W.A. Mozart's Sämtliche Werke*, published by Breitkopf and Härtel (1876–1905). Originally set for a baritone soloist with an accompaniment of flute, bassoon and strings, this edition of "*Non siate ritrosi*" includes a keyboard reduction of the instrumental parts. Dynamic and metronomic indications and optional English words have also been added by the editor. Additionally, it has been transposed up a major second from the original key of G major.

This exuberant and humorous aria should be performed with great energy, always emphasizing the naturally energized syllables of the original Italian words to emphatically convey the rather humorous descriptions of their qualities as men.

PRONUNCIATION GUIDE

Non sia-te ri-tro-si oc-chiet-ti vez-zo-si,
nɔn sja-te ri-<u>tro</u>-zi ok:kjet:ti vet:<u>tso</u>-zi,

due lam-pi͜a-mo-ro-si vi-bra-te͜un po quà.
due <u>lam</u>-pia-mo-<u>ro</u>-zi vi-<u>bra</u>-tεun pɔ kwɑ.

Fe-li-ci ren-de-te-ci, a-ma-te con no-i,
fe-<u>li</u>-tʃi rεn-<u>de</u>-te-tʃi a-<u>ma</u>-tε kɔn <u>nɔ</u>-i,

e no-i fe-li-cis-si-me fa-re-mo͜an-che vo-i.
e <u>nɔ</u>-i fe-li-tʃis-si-mε fa-<u>rε</u>-mɔan-kε <u>vɔ</u>-i.

Guar-da-te, toc-ca-te, il tut-to͜os-ser-va-te;
gwar-<u>da</u>-tε tɔk:<u>ka</u>-tε, il <u>tut</u>:tɔ-sεr-<u>va</u>-tε;

siam due ca-ri mat-ti, siam for-ti͜e ben fat-ti,
sjɑm duε <u>ka</u>-ri <u>mat</u>:ti, sjɑm <u>for</u>-tje ben <u>fat</u>:ti,

e co-me͜o-gnum ve-de, sia mer-to,
e <u>kɔ</u>-mεɔ-ɲjum <u>ve</u>-de, siɑ <u>mεr</u>-tɔ,

sia ca-so, ab-bia-mo bel pie-de,
siɑ <u>ka</u>-zɔ, ab:<u>bja</u>-mɔ bεl <u>pjε</u>-dε,

bell' oc-chio, bel na-so, guar-da-te bel pie-de,
bεl:<u>lɔk</u>:kjɔ, bεl <u>na</u>-sɔ, gwar-<u>da</u>-tε bεl <u>pjε</u>-dε,

os-ser-va-te bell' oc-chio, toc-ca-te bel na-so,
os-sεr-<u>va</u>-tε bεl:<u>lok</u>:kjɔ, tɔk:<u>ka</u>-tε bεl <u>na</u>-sɔ,

il tut-to͜os-ser-va-te:
il <u>tut</u>:tɔs-sεr-<u>va</u>-tεː

e que-sti mu-stac-chi chia-ma-re si pos-so-no tri-on-fi de-gli͜uo-mi-ni, pen-nac-chi d'a-mor,
e <u>kwe</u>-sti mu-<u>stak</u>:ki kjа-<u>ma</u>-rε si pɔ-<u>so</u>-no tri-<u>on</u>-fi de-<u>ʎiwɔ</u>-mi-ni, pεn:<u>nak</u>:ki dа-<u>mor</u>,

tri-on-fi de-gli͜uo-mi-ni, pen-nac-chi d'a-mor, tri-on-fi, pen-nac-chi, mu-stac-chi!
tri-<u>on</u>-fi de-<u>ʎiwɔ</u>-mi-ni, pεn:<u>nak</u>:ki dа-<u>mor</u>, tri-<u>on</u>-fi, pεn:<u>nak</u>:ki, mu-<u>stak</u>:ki!

Footnotes to Italian Pronunciation

- In multiple syllable words, the syllables that should be stressed are underlined.

- [ɲ] indicates that the tip of the tongue should be in contact with the lower front teeth while the front of the tongue is raised and pressed against the front of the hard palate. Nasality is then produced when breath passes through the nose.

- [ɾ] should be flipped.

- [r] should be trilled.

- [ʎ] indicates a similar sound to [lj] in the word "million" [mi-ljən], requiring only one tongue action, as in the word "degli" [de-ʎi].

- Certain double consonants can be sustained on a pitch while maintaining a legato line, such as those in the word "pennachi." The singer should take time for the singable double consonants in each of these words from the preceding musical note.

- There are other double consonants, such as those in the words "occhietti" and "vezzosi," which interrupt the legato line when pronounced correctly. For example, when singing the word "occhietti" [ok:kjet:ti], the singer should briefly stop on the first [k], creating a slight silence before the sounding of the second [k].

TRANSLATION

Do not be shy, pretty little eyes,
Send over here two flashing, loving glances.
And we, being the happiest of men, will make you very happy too.
Look, touch, observe everything,
We are two dear madmen, we are strong and well built;
And as everyone can see, be it merit, be it chance,
We have pretty feet, lovely eyes, a good nose,
And these mustaches can be called triumphs of manhood, plumes of love,
Triumphs, plumes, mustaches!

6. Non siate ritrosi

(Oh, Don't You Be Shy)

Italian words by
LORENZO DE PONTE (1749-1838)
English words by **PATRICK M. LIEBERGEN**

from COSÌ FAN TUTTE
Music by **WOLFGANG AMADEUS MOZART** (1756-1791)
Edited and Arranged by **PATRICK M. LIEBERGEN**

no - i, e no i fe - li - cis - si - me fa - re - mo an - che
beg_____you, and we shall bring great hap - pi - ness to you_____ now and

vo - i. Guar - da - te, toc - ca - te, il tut - to os - ser -
ev - er. Look at us, and touch us, and treat us with

va - te; siam due ca - ri mat - ti, siam for - ti e ben
fa - vor; we are two dear mad - men, so strong,_____ full of

va - te bell' oc - chio, toc - ca - te bel
serve all we bring you, and touch us, each

na - so, il tut - to os - ser - va - te: e
fine nose, and treat us with fa - vor: we

que - sti mu - stac - chi chia - ma - re si pos - so - no tri -
have nice mus - tach - es, they bring___ us great tri - umph, they

O mio babbino caro
(O My Beloved Father)

Giacomo Puccini (1858–1924)

Born into a musical family in Luca, Tuscany, Giacomo Puccini was the most important Italian opera composer in the generation after Giuseppe Verdi. Known mainly for his operas, Puccini also wrote some orchestral pieces, sacred music, chamber music and songs for voice and piano. Puccini became especially popular because of his melodic writing, dramatic harmonies and achieving effective drama, balancing action and conflict with moments of repose, contemplation and lyricism.

He first studied music with his uncle, Fortunato Magi, and with the director of the *Instituto Musicale Pacini*, Carlo Angeloni, before starting his career at the age of fourteen as an organist in Lucca. It was after Puccini heard Verdi's *Aïda* at Pisa in 1876 that he became inspired to write operas. Deciding to follow his instinct for operatic composition, Puccini went to study at the Milan Conservatory in 1880. He completed his first opera, *Le Villi*, in 1884 when he was a student in order to enter a competition for a one-act opera. Although he didn't win, the publisher Giulio Ricordi arranged for a successful production of it at the *Teatro Dal Verme*. *Edgar*, his next opera, was a failure. However, *Manon Lescaut*, his third opera, which he competed in 1893, brought him international recognition. The two librettists, Luigi Illica and Giuseppe Giacos, who collaborated with Puccini on *Manon Lescaut*, also provided him the librettos for the three most successful operas of the early twentieth century: *La Bohème* (1896), *Tosca* (1900) and *Madama Butterfly* (1904). *The Girl of the Golden West* (1910) is another of his mature operas.

Puccini was associated with a movement known as *verismo* (realism), which involved selecting subjects from everyday life and treating them in a down-to-earth fashion. His *La Bohème* (1896) and *Tosca* (1900) are his most famous operas in this tradition. Although *verismo* was a short-lived movement, some of the best-loved works in the operatic repertory were produced by other leading operatic composers, such as Mascagni and Leoncavallo, who followed the tenants of that movement.

Puccini's early successes were followed by prosperity and some very unfortunate incidents, such as a serious car crash and accusations of infedelity from his wife. However, he continued to compose inspired works. Among them was *Il Trittico (The Trilogy)*, which premiered in New York in 1918. Commissioned by the Metropolitan Opera, the work is composed of three-one-act operas: *Il Tabarro*, *Suor Angelica* and *Gianni Schicchi*, one of his best-loved masterpieces.

Turandot, Puccini's last of his twelve operas, was left unfinished because he died before he could complete the last portion. When Arturo Toscanini conducted the premiere performance in 1926 to a sold-out crowd with Benito Mussolini in attendance, the performance was stopped at the point where Puccini had completed the score. The conductor then turned to the audience to explain that they had just heard all that was completed by the composer and that Puccini had written no more.

The comedy *Gianni Schicchi* is set in Florence in the year 1299. The action begins in a large bedroom in the house of Buoso Donati, a rich Florentine, who has just died. The relatives cease their mourning and quarrel when they discover that Donati's money has been willed to the church. Rinuccio, nephew to the dead Donati, is in love with Lauretta but is forbiden by his aunt Zito to marry her because she has no dowry. He therefore sends for Lauretta and her father Gianni Schicchi so that Gianni can possibly help them marry. When Lauretta and Gianni Schicchi enter the scene, there is an argument between all, provoking Lauretta's father to attempt to leave. However, Lauretta stops him with her performance of "*O mio babbino caro*," singing that she loves Rinuccio and if her father doesn't help them, she will throw herself in the river and die. The "Ponte Vecchio" in the libretto refers to the famous old bridge in Florence, Italy.

This beautifully simple and tuneful aria is accompanied in Puccini's original score by woodwinds, horns, trumpets, harp and strings. A keyboard reduction of those parts is included here, along with the original Italian words by Giovacchino Forzana. Tempo and dynamic indications and optional English words have also been added to this score. This edition features the aria in its original key.

"*O mio babbino caro*" should be sung very smoothly and freely while expressing the natural ebb and flow of the tuneful melodic lines.

PRONUNCIATION GUIDE

O mio bab-bi-no ca-ro,
o mi<ɔ> bab:<u>bi</u>-n<ɔ> <u>ka</u>-rɔ,

mi pia-ce, è bel-lo, bel-lo;
mi pja-tʃɛ <u>bɛl</u>:lɔ, <u>bɛl</u>:lɔ;

vo'an-da-re in Porta Ros-sa a com-per-ar l'a nel-lo!
vɔan-<u>da</u>-rɛin <u>pɔr</u>-ta <u>ros</u>-sa ɑ kom-per-<u>ar</u> la <u>nɛl</u>:lɔ!

Sì, sì, ci vo-glio an-da-re!
si, si, tʃi <u>vɔ</u>-ʎɔan-<u>da</u>-rɛ!

e se l'a-mas-si in-dar-no,
e sɛ la-<u>mas</u>-sin-<u>dar</u>-nɔ,

an-drei sul Pon-te Vec-chio,
an-<u>drɛi</u> sul <u>pon</u>-tɛ <u>vɛk</u>:kjɔ,

ma per but-tar-mi in Ar-no!
ma per but:<u>tar</u>-min <u>ar</u>-nɔ!

Mi strug-go e mi tor-men-to!
mi <u>strug</u>:gɔe mi tɔr-<u>men</u>-tɔ!

O Di-o, vor-rei mo-rir!
o <u>di</u>-ɔ, vɔr:<u>rɛi</u> mo-<u>rir</u>!

Bab-bo, pie-tà, pie-tà!
<u>bab</u>:bɔ pje-<u>ta</u>, pje-<u>ta</u>!

Footnotes to Italian Pronunciation

- In multiple syllable words, the syllables that should be stressed are underlined.

- [ɾ] should be flipped.

- [r] should be trilled.

- [rː] has the length of two trilled r's, one to be sung on the pitch of the preceding vowel, the other on the pitch of the following vowel. There should be no break.

- [ʎ] indicates a similar sound to [lj] in the word "million" [<u>mi</u>-ljən], requiring only one tongue action, as in the word "voglio" [<u>vɔ</u>-ʎɔ].

- Certain double consonants can be sustained on a pitch while maintaining a legato line, such as those in the words "bello" and "nello." The singer should take time for the singable double consonants in each of these words from the preceding musical note.

- There are other double consonants, such as those in the words "babbino" and "Vecchio," which interrupt the legato line when pronounced correctly. For example, when singing the word "babbino" [bab:<u>bi</u>-nɔ], the singer should briefly stop on the first [b], creating a slight silence before the sounding of the second [b].

TRANSLATION

Oh my dear daddy,
he pleases me and he is handsome;
I want to go to Porta Rossa to buy the ring!
Yes, yes, I want to go there!
And if my love were in vain, I would go to the Ponte Vecchio,
and throw myself into the Arno!
I suffer and I am tormented! Oh God, I want to die!
Daddy, have pity, have pity!

7. O mio babbino caro

(O My Beloved Father)

Italian words by
GIOVACCHINO FORZANO (1884-1970)
English words by
PATRICK M. LIEBERGEN

from GIANNI SCHICCHI
Music by **GIACOMO PUCCINI** (1858-1924)
Edited and Arranged by
PATRICK M. LIEBERGEN

Smoothly and freely (♪ = ca. 84)

O mio bab - bi - no caro, mi pia - ce, è bel - lo, bel - lo; vo'an -
O my be - lov - ed fa - ther, he pleas - es me, I love him; I'll

da - re_in Por - ta Ros - sa a com-per - ar l'a
go to Por - ta Ros - sa to buy the ring, please

nel - lo! Sì, sì, ci vo-glio_an - da - re!
let - me! Oh yes, I want to go - there!

e se l'a-mas-si_in - dar - no, an - drei sul Pon - te
And if my love were hope - less, I'd go to Pon - te

Bab - bo, pie - tà,   pie - tà,
Fa - ther, here me,   hear   me,

bab - bo, pie - tà,   pie - tà!
fa - ther, hear me,   hear   me!

O Rest in the Lord

Felix Mendelssohn (1809–1847)

In his brief life of only thirty-eight years, Felix Mendelssohn composed a great amount of music in most of the instrumental and vocal forms of his time. Born into a privileged family in Hamburg, Germany, he had many excellent experiences as a performer, composer and conductor at a very early age. During his lifetime, Mendelssohn traveled widely to many countries for his composing and conducting assignments. He went to England ten times and was once entertained at Buckingham Palace by Queen Victoria.

Mendelssohn's training in the music of Bach, Handel and Mozart greatly contributed to his development as a composer. In fact, Mendelssohn is credited with revitalizing the music of Johann Sebastian Bach. When he conducted Bach's *St. Matthew Passion* in 1829, it was the first performance of that work since Bach's death seventy-nine years before. Mendelssohn's knowledge of the techniques and materials of past masters is evident in much of his creative output, particularly in his choral works.

Mendelssohn's choral works are among his greatest achievements as a composer. His oratorios, particularly *St. Paul* and *Elijah*, are highly regarded for their great appeal to performers and audiences alike. Composed for four soloists, an S.A.T.B. choir with incidental solo singers and orchestra, *Elijah* was first conducted by Mendelssohn in 1846 for the Birmingham Festival in England. Originally written in German, the oratorio is usually heard today in Mendelssohn's English version. It is based upon the Old Testament story (I Kings 17) of Elijah, a prophet who predicts three years of drought because the children of Israel have turned away from God ("Yahweh").

"O Rest in the Lord" appears in the second part of the oratorio in response to Elijah's discouragement. After Elijah becomes very low in spirit and asks for death, an angel brings comfort to him with this aria. One of the best known solos from *Elijah*, "O Rest in the Lord" is normally performed by an alto in the presentation of this large-scale work. In this edition, this solo has been transposed up a minor third from the original key.

The keyboard accompaniment of "O Rest in the Lord" is a reduction of the original instrumental parts. The editor has also contributed tempo and dynamic indications.

8. O Rest in the Lord

Psalm 37

from ELIJAH
Music by **FELIX MENDELSSOHN** (1809-1847)
Edited and Arranged by **PATRICK M. LIEBERGEN**

give thee thy heart's de - sires. Com-mit thy way un - to Him,_____ and trust in

Him; com-mit thy way un - to Him,_____ and trust in Him, and fret_____ not thy-

self_____ be-cause of e - vil do - ers. O rest in the Lord, wait pa-tient-ly for

Him, wait pa-tient-ly for Him; O rest in the Lord, wait pa-tient-ly for

Him, and He shall give thee thy heart's de-sires, and He shall

give thee thy heart's de-sires, and He shall give thee thy heart's de-

sires. O rest in the Lord, O rest in the Lord, and wait,____

____ wait____ pa-tient-ly for Him.

Ombra mai fù
(Lovely and Sweet)

George Frideric Handel (1685–1759)

"*Ombra mai fù*" is the opening aria in the opera *Serse* (*Xerxes*), HWV 40. It is sung in the first scene of the opera by the main character, King Serse, who is in love with a tree. Lounging in his garden, he sings in praise of a tree's shade as he sits beneath it. A number of love relationships between the main characters are then presented in the opera, with Serse first becoming determined to wed Romilda. Composed in the popular form of the time, opera seria, *Serse* is based on a serious subject and involves characters from ancient history. In accordance with this type of production, *Serse* is set in Persia in 450 B.C.

First performed in London in 1738, *Serse* was not an immediate success. Despite the great amount of beautiful music, it was withdrawn from London's Haymarket Theatre after only five performances and was rarely performed until it was rediscovered in the nineteenth century. Now considered one of his finest operas, there has been a renewed interest in it with recordings and stage productions in recent years.

"*Ombra mai fù*" is one of Handel's best known melodies, and has appeared in numerous vocal and instrumental settings. It is often called "Handel's *Largo*," although the tempo of "*larghetto*" appears in the original score. The aria at the time of its first production was performed by a castrato, a type of singer who had an unnaturally high adult male voice. Since the practice of employing castrato has been abandoned, the part of Serse is usually sung today by a woman or sometimes a countertenor (male falsettist).

The source for this edition is *George Friedrich Händels Werke*, Volume 92, published by Breitkopf and Härtel (1892). Scored originally for an orchestral accompaniment of strings and continuo in the key of F major, this edition includes a keyboard reduction of those parts as the accompaniment. Tempo and dynamic indications, the fermatas in the last measure and optional English words have also been added. "*Ombra mai fù*" should be performed very smoothly and slowly while maintaining a constant quarter note pulse.

PRONUNCIATION GUIDE

Om-bra mai fù
ɔm-bra mɑi fu

di ve-ge-ta-bi-le
di ve-dʒe-tɑ-bi-lɛ

ca-ra ed a-ma-bi-le so-a-ve più.
cɑ-rɑed ɑ-mɑ-bi-lɛ so-ɑ-vɛ pju.

Footnotes to Italian Pronunciation

- In multiple syllable words, the syllables that should be stressed are underlined.
- [ɾ] should be flipped.
- [r] should be trilled.

TRANSLATION

Never was there a shade of vegetation,
more dear, amiable,
and sweet.

9. Ombra mai fù

(Lovely and Sweet)

Italian words based upon librettos by
SILVIO STAMPIGLIA (1664–1725) *and*
FRANCESCO CAVALLI (1602–1676)
English words by **PATRICK M. LIEBERGEN**

from SERSE
Music by
GEORGE FRIDERIC HANDEL (1685–1759)
Edited by **PATRICK M. LIEBERGEN**

Sheep May Safely Graze
(Schafe können sicher weiden)

Johann Sebastian Bach (1685–1750)

Johann Sebastian Bach was a musical genius who lived at the end of the Baroque era. Recognized as one of the greatest composers of all time, he wrote in almost every musical genre of his time and was especially successful at contrapuntal technique.

Born into a large family of musicians, Bach spent his entire life in the Thuringia area of Germany. After early training in organ and violin, he performed as an organist in Arnstadt and Mülhausen. During his subsequent assignment as court organist and chamber musician to the Duke of Weimar, Bach wrote most of his finest organ works and a number of sacred and secular works. Moving to Cöthen, he wrote his chief orchestral and chamber music works as Kapellmeister and Director of Chamber Music for the Prince of Anhalt.

In 1722, Bach was appointed Cantor at St. Thomas' Church in Leipzig, where he spent his remaining years composing most of his great church music. It was in Leipzig that he completed the majority of his chorale cantatas, which were required for use in the Lutheran worship services and other occasions. Bach's chorale cantatas typically incorporated Lutheran chorale tunes in settings for soloists, choir and orchestra. Their texts were usually adapted from the Bible, the Lutheran service and hymns or chorales. Bach was a master at combining the music and words of a cantata to highlight the scriptural texts and sermon themes prescribed for certain days.

Bach received a number of outside commissions and engagements during his career. His first notable commission was from Weimar's Duke Wilhelm Ernst to produce a secular cantata for the birthday celebration of Duke Christian of Saxe-Weissenfels. For this event on February 23, 1713, Bach wrote *Was mir behagt, ist nur die muntre Jagd* ("The merry hunt is my one delight"), BWV 208.

Since Duke Christian was a very avid hunter, Bach used a libretto by Salamo Franck based on mythological subjects which praised the sport while expressing good wishes for the Duke. Franck was then the secretary to the court at Weimar and would eventually provide Bach with numerous sacred cantata texts in his Weimar years.

Bach's efforts resulted in a very successful cantata of joyful energy and colorful orchestration. Three of its movements were later used as parodies in his church cantatas composed in Leipzig. Bach's secular cantatas were composed in the same style as his sacred cantatas, except for the absence of chorales. Bach wrote about 40 secular cantatas for special occasions, including weddings and ceremonies.

"Sheep May Safely Graze" appears in the tenth movement of Bach's cantata No. 208. Originally scored for soprano solo, two treble recorders and continuo in B-flat major, this edition in G major provides a keyboard accompaniment based on the solo and instrumental parts. The original recorder parts are provided for performance by flutes or other C-instruments. Dynamics and tempo indications and the well known English text by Katherine K. Davis have also been included in this edition.

In performance, the pastoral mood suggested by the melody and words should be conveyed with energetic and legato singing, and the tempo should remain constant throughout the work, with a slight ritard just before the end of the piece. In keeping with the performance practice of Bach's music, vocal ornamentation may be added in accordance with musical factors, such as the melodic line and tempo, and the ability of the performer.

In this movement, Bach indicated "tr" over three notes which should be ornamented. In measure 6, for example, the singer may choose to perform a rather easy mordent or a more challenging trill, as follows:

Measure 6 mordent

Measure 6 trill

The mordent shown in the bracket may also be sung as two thirty-second notes followed by a dotted eighth note. In singing the trill, it is customary for the singer to begin

singing on the beat and for the ornament to begin on the upper note as shown in the bracket. It is also possible to occasionally add ornamentation not originally indicated in the score, such as trills at cadence points. In addition, the singer may add notes in measures 10 (and 50) and 32 as shown in brackets in the following examples:

Measure 10

Measure 32

For more information on ornamentation, please see *Ornamentation: A Question and Answer Manual*, by Valery Lloyd-Watts and Carole L. Bigler (published by Alfred Publishing Company, No. 6000).

PRONUNCIATION GUIDE

Scha-fe kön-nen si-cher wei-den,
ʃa-fə kœ-nən zɪ-hər vɑɪ-dən,

wo ein gu-ter Hir-te wacht.
vo aɪn guː-tər hɪr-tə vaxt.

Wo Re-gen-ten wohl re-gie-ren,
voː re-gɛn-tən vol re-giː-rən,

kann man Ruh' und Frie-den spü-ren,
kɑn man ru ʊnt friː-dən ʃpyː-rən,

und was Län-der glück-lich macht.
ʊnt vɑs lɛn-dər glyk-lɪç maxt.

Footnotes to German Pronunciation

- In multiple syllable words, the syllables that should be stressed are underlined.

- [ɾ] should be flipped.

TRANSLATION

Sheep can safely graze where a good shepherd watches.
Where rulers reign well, one feels peace and quiet,
and what makes the lands happy.

10. Sheep May Safely Graze

(Schafe können sicher weiden)

with optional two flutes*

German words by
SALOMO FRANCK (1659–1725)
English words by **KATHERINE K. DAVIS** (1892–1980)

from WAS MIR BEHAGT, IST NUR DIE MUNTRE JAGD
Music by **JOHANN SEBASTIAN BACH** (1685-1750)
Edited and Arranged by **PATRICK M. LIEBERGEN**

*Flute parts are on pages 115–116.

Those who rule, with wis - dom guid - ing,_____
Wo Re - gen - ten wohl re - gie - ren,_____

bring to_____ hearts a peace a - bid - ing,_____
kann man_____ Ruh' und Frie - den_____ spü - ren,

bless   a   land   with___   joy   made___   bright.
und   a   was   Län - der___   glück - lich___   macht.

Those   who___
Wo   Re -

Sheep may___ safe___ ly graze and___ pas - ture___
Scha - fe___ kön___ nen si - cher___ wei - den,___

in___ a___ watch - ful shep - herd's___ sight.
wo___ ein___ gu - ter Hir - te___ wacht.

in___ a___ watch - ful shep - herd's
wo___ ein___ gu - ter Hir - te___

sight.
wacht.

Sorry Her Lot

Arthur Sullivan (1842–1900)

Gilbert and Sullivan refers to the partnership of librettist W.S. Gilbert and composer Arthur Sullivan, who together wrote fourteen comic operas between 1871 and 1896 for London audiences. Their twenty-five year partnership began when they were commissioned by John Hollingshead to create the burlesque *Thespis, or the Gods Grown Old* for entertainment during the Christmas season at the Gaiety Theatre. They scored their first big hit four years later with the comic opera *Trial By Jury*, which debuted at the Royalty Theatre in London in 1875. The next three works, *The Sorcerer*, *H.M.S. Pinafore* and *The Pirates of Penzance*, were performed at the Opéra Comique. After their manager built the new Savoy Theatre in 1881 for their productions, they continued to produce dramatic works, which came to be known as the "Savoy Operas." *Iolanthe*, composed in 1882, was the first of their works to premiere at the new theatre. However, a quarrel during the run of *The Gondoliers* eventually destroyed their partnership, when Gilbert expressed his concern about the excessive cost of the carpets for the lobby of the Savoy. Gilbert's argument with the manager of the theatre, Richard D'Oyly Carte, and Sullivan was really over the ability of Carte to make judicious decisions regarding the finances of their partnership. Although the working relationship of Gilbert and Sullivan eventually stopped, their operas continued to achieve international acclaim, and they are performed today. It was Gilbert's creative lyrics, with absurd situations culminating in logical conclusions, combined with Sullivan's memorable melodies full of humor and pathos that led to their tremendous success.

Born in London, Sir William Schwenck Gilbert was an English dramatist, librettist, poet and illustrator. He completed the "Bab Ballads," an extensive collection of light verse accompanied by his own comical drawings, in addition to over seventy-five plays and libretti, numerous stories, poems, lyrics and additional comic and serious pieces. Educated at King's College, London and Oxford, he was interested in the theatre from an early age. With an incredible output of farces, operetta librettos, adaptations of novels and translations of French drama, he was a highly respected writer, and a director, before he ultimately teamed up with Authur Sullivan. At the height of success with Sullivan, Gilbert not only directed and oversaw all aspects of production; he also designed the costumes himself for *Patience*, *Iolanthe*, *Princess Ida* and *Ruddigore*. After the break-up of the collaboration, Gilbert's creative powers were in decline. He then went into semi-retirement, completing more writing projects and plays. He died of heart failure in 1911 as a result of trying to rescue someone in his lake.

Also born in London, Sir Arthur Seymour Sullivan was an English composer, conductor and organist. Best known for his operatic collaborations with W.S. Gilbert, his output included operas, orchestral works, choral works, two ballets, incidental music to several plays and numerous hymns and other church pieces, songs, parlous ballads, part songs, carols and piano chamber pieces. Admitted to the choir of the Chapel Royal as a young man and educated at the Royal Academy of Music and the Leipzig Conservatory, he went on to compose major orchestral and choral works while showing an affinity for theatrical composition. Even during his numerous operatic successes with W.S. Gilbert, he continued his career as a conductor and educator. Besides the comic operas, his most successful large-scale work was his oratorio *The Golden Legend*. After his break-up with Gilbert, Sullivan continued to write dramatic and ballet works. He died of pneumonia at the age of fifty-eight, and was buried in St. Paul Cathedral by order of the Queen.

"Sorry Her Lot" is a slow, plaintive aria performed by Josephine in the 1878 opera *H.M.S. Pinafore*. This opera ran for 571 performances and became incredibly popular in England, as well as in the United States. The theme of *H.M.S. Pinafore* is the problem created by love between members of different social classes. In this drama the Captain of the Pinafore does not know that his daughter has fallen in love with a common sailor serving on her father's ship. Meanwhile, the Captain has arranged for her to marry the First Lord of the Admiralty, Sir Joseph Porter. It also seems that Little Buttercup, a dockside vendor in Portsmouth, has a romantic interest in the Captain. In the tradition of Gilbert and Sullivan, it all works out in the end.

When Josephine makes her entrance on stage, she expresses her sorrow in "Sorry Her Lot" at the situation in which she is trapped. She loves Ralph, who is a sailor aboard the Pinafore. However, as the daughter of a captain, her social position is far above that of a sailor. She fears that this class difference will prevent their love from ever being accepted. She therefore sadly sings that "hope is dead" aboard her father's ship, the Pinafore.

This edition appears a minor second lower than the original key. Additionally, tempo and dynamic indications have been included in this version.

11. Sorry Her Lot

Words by
WILLIAM GILBERT (1836–1911)

from H.M.S. PINAFORE
Music by **ARTHUR SULLIVAN** (1842–1900)
Edited by **PATRICK M. LIEBERGEN**

own the spell ut-tered by eyes_____ that speak too plain - ly.

Sor - ry her lot_____ who loves__ too well, heav - y the heart that hopes but vain - ly.

Heav - y the sor - row that bows_____ the head when love is a -

Time To Say Goodbye
(Con te partiró)

Francesco Sartori (1957–)

"Time To Say Goodbye" is an operatic pop song, composed by the Italian composer, pianist and trumpet player Francesco Sartori with Italian words by Lucio Quarantotto and English words by Frank Peterson. Known originally as *"Con te partiró,"* it was premiered by Andrea Bocelli at the 1995 San Remo Festival, a prestigious singing competition in Italy. When the original solo version was featured later that year in his album titled *Bocelli*, it immediately became very popular in Europe with massive sales.

The internationally renowned Sarah Brightman eventually contacted Bocelli after she heard that recording, requesting to perform another version of the song with him. With the title of the song changed from *"Con te partiró"* (I'll go with you) to "Time To Say Goodbye," they debuted their duet in 1996 as a farewell song at the last bout of Henry Maske, the German World Light-Heavyweight boxing champion. Bocelli and Brightman then recorded it with the London Symphony Orchestra. Also in 1996,

Bocelli's album *Romanza* was released, which contains both the original solo *"Con te partiró"* and the duet "Time To Say Goodbye" with Brightman.

"Time To Say Goodbye" has continued to appear on recordings by Bocelli, Brightman and numerous other vocalists, and it has also been heard in film, television, sporting events, concerts and additional venues.

Each of the two verses includes an opening portion which should be sung quietly, slowly and freely in parlando style. For example, in the first ten measures of the first verse, the voice should maintain a freedom while gently slowing to sound the quarter notes in measures 6, 8 and 9. The "a tempo" indication in measures 15 and 32 of the respective first and second verses signals that the singer and accompanist should sound the rhythmic figures in a more constant beat. Those latter sections should be performed very majestically while the voice rings with brilliance and emotion.

TRANSLATION

When I'm alone I dream on the horizon and words fail;
yes, I know there is no light in a room where the sun is absent,
if you are not with me.
At the windows show everyone my heart, which you set alight;
Enclose within me the light you encountered on the street.

Time to say goodbye, (Con te partiró—I'll go with you,)
to countries I never saw and shared with you,
now, yes, I shall experience them.
I'll go with you on ships across seas, which, I know,
no, no, exist no longer;
with you I shall experience them.

When you are far away I dream on the horizon and words fail,
and, yes, I know that you are with me;
you, my moon, are here with me,
my sun, you are here with me.

Time to say goodbye, (Con te partiró—I'll go with you,)
to countries I never saw and shared with you,
now, yes, I shall experience them.
I'll go with you on ships across seas, which, I know,
no, no, exist no longer;
with you I shall experience them again.
I'll go with you on ships across seas, which, I know,
no, no, exist no longer;
with you I shall experience them again.
I'll go with you,
I with you.

PRONUNCIATION GUIDE

Quan-do so-no so-lo so-gno‿al-l'o-riz-zon-te‿e man-can le pa-ro-le,
kwan-dɔ so-nɔ so-lɔ so-ɲɔal-lɔ-ridːdzon-te man-kan le pɑ-rɔ-lɛ,

sì lo so che non c'è lu-ce‿in u-na stan-za quan-do man-ca‿il so-le
si lɔ sɔ kɛ nɔn kɛ lu-tʃein u-na stan-tsa kwan-tɔ man-kail sɔ-lɛ

se non ci sei tu con me, con me.
sɛ nɔn ki sɛi tu kɔn me, kɔn me.

Su le fe-ne-stre mo-stra‿a tut-ti‿il mio cuo-re che hai ac-ce-so
su le fɛ-nɛ-strɛ mo-stra tutːtil miɔ kwɔ-rɛ kɛ hai atːtʃɛ-sɔ

chiu-di den-tro me la lu-ce che hai‿in con-tra-to per stra-da.
kju-di den-trɔ me la lu-tʃɛ kɛ hain kɔn-tra-tɔ per stra-da.

Pa-e-si che non ho mai ve-du-to‿e vis-su-to con te
pɑ-ɛ-si kɛ nɔn hɔ mai ve-du-tɔe vis-su-tɔ kɔn te

a-des-so sì li vi-vrò con te par-ti-rò
ɑ-des-sɔ si li vi-vrɔ kɔn te pɑr-ti-rɔ

su na-vi per ma-ri che io lo so no no non e-si-sto-no più con te io li vi-vrò.
su na-vi per ma-ri kɛ jɔ lɔ sɔ nɔ nɔ nɔn e-zi-stɔ-nɔ pju kɔn te iɔ li-vi-vrɔ.

Quan-do sei lon-ta-na so-gno‿al-l'o-riz-zon-te‿e man-can le pa-ro-le,
kwan-dɔ sɛi lon-ta-na so-ɲual-lɔ-ridːdzon-tɛ man-kan le pɑ-rɔ-lɛ,

e io sì lo so che sei con me, con me.
e io si lɔ sɔ kɛ sɛi kɔn me, kɔn me.

Tu mia lu-na tu sei qui con me
tu miɑ lu-na tu sɛi kwi kɔn me

mi-o so-le tu sei qui con me, con me, con me, con me.
mi-ɔ so-lɛ tu sɛi kwi kɔn me, kɔn me, kɔn me, kɔn me.

Footnotes to Italian Pronunciation

- In multiple syllable words, the syllables that should be stressed are underlined.

- [ɲ] indicates that the tip of the tongue should be in contact with the lower front teeth while the front of the tongue is raised and pressed against the front of the hard palate. Nasality is then produced when breath passes through the nose.

- [ɾ] should be flipped.

- [r] should be trilled.

- Certain double consonants can by sustained on a pitch while maintaining a legato line such as the double "l" in "all'orizzonte." The singer should take time for the singable double consonants from the preceding musical note.

- There are other double consonants, such as those in the words "orizzonte" and "accesso," which interrupt the legato line when pronounced correctly. For example, when singing the word "orizzonte" [ɔ-ridːdzon-tɛ], the singer should briefly stop on the [d], creating a slight silence before the sounding of the [dz].

12. Time To Say Goodbye

(Con Te Partiró)

Italian lyrics by
LUCIO QUARANTOTTO
English lyrics by
FRANK PETERSON

Music by
FRANCESCO SARTORI
Edited and Arranged by
PATRICK M. LIEBERGEN

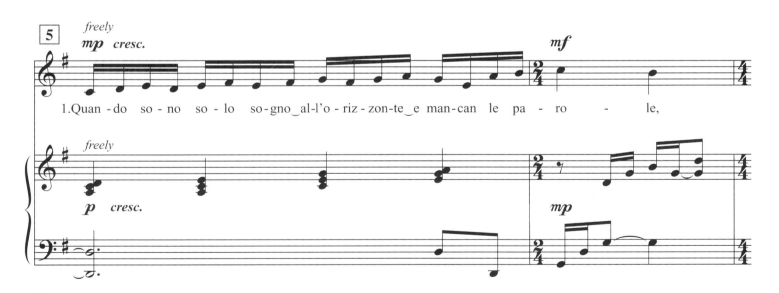

na - vi per ma - ri che io lo so no no non e - si - sto - no

più con te io li ri vi - vrò con te par - ti -

rò_____ su na - vi per ma - ri che io lo

so no no non e - si - sto - no più con te io li ri vi -

vrò con te   par - ti - rò.

Io con

te.

Voi che sapete
(You Know What Love Is)

Wolfgang Amadeus Mozart (1756–1791)

"*Voi che sapete*" is a very popular aria from Mozart's *Le nozze di Figaro (The Marriage of Figaro)*, one of the most beloved and performed operas in today's standard repertoire. This opera buffa was composed in 1786, with an Italian libretto by Lorenzo da Ponte, based on a 1784 stage comedy by Pierre Beaumarchais, *La folle journée, ou, le Mariage de Figaro*. Beaumarchais's play is the second in his Figaro trilogy of plays, and follows the action of his first comedy *Le Barbier de Séville (The Barber of Seville)*. Both Beaumarchais's plays *The Barber of Seville* and *The Marriage of Figaro* are examples of light comedy in the eighteenth century, but are now remembered by the respective operas of Rossini and Mozart.

The plays were considered scandalous at the time because the drama involves an incompetent nobleman being upstaged by a crafty, quick-witted servant in their quest for the same woman. Performances were opposed by King Louis XVI and the French censors, and in Austria, Emperor Joseph II allowed Mozart to set it to music only after all the political speeches were taken out. The first performances of *Le nozze di Figaro* in Vienna and Prague were enthusiastically received, despite the fact that a servant's name—Figaro—appeared in the title. With its humorous wordplay and lively characterization, Mozart's setting of Beaumarchais's play signaled the impending decline of the aristocracy, when the victory of ability over birthright was triumphed by the hero Figaro.

The action of *Le nozze di Figaro* recounts a single day in the palace of the Count Almaviva, where he lives with his Countess and a number of dependents. Among these are Figaro, Figaro's fiancée Susanna (the Countess's maid) and the Count's page, Cherubino. Rather than featuring a well-defined plot, the opera is a series of awkward and humorous situations, complete with a vibrant dialogue between the individuals involved. It is about the struggles and reconciliation of those in the court, all of which are presented in a masterpiece of comedic sentiment with inspired melodies and rich orchestrations.

"*Voi che sapete*" is performed by Cherubino, who is about to be sent off to the army because the Count finds him a nuisance. When Cherubino appears before the Countess and Susanna in the second act to tell them his fate, this aria is sung at the request of Susanna for a love song. Cherubino is characterized as a young adolescent who is in love with every woman he meets, and because his voice is yet unbroken, is always played by a female singer.

W.A. Mozart's Sämtliche Werke, V, published by Breitkopf and Härtel (1876–1905) is the source for this edition. Originally set for mezzo-soprano with an accompaniment of woodwinds, horns and strings, the keyboard accompaniment in this arrangement is a reduction of those instrumental parts. Presented here in the original key, dynamic and metronomic indications and optional English words have also been added by the editor.

Mozart's very tuneful melody is first heard in the opening measures of the accompaniment, where it should be given emphasis against the backdrop of the inner pulsating sixteenth notes. Both keyboard and vocal parts should be performed lightly with two constant beats per measure. The naturally energized syllables should be clearly pronounced while closely following the suggested dynamics that highlight the contrasting phrases.

PRONUNCIATION GUIDE

Voi che sa-pe-te che co-sa‿è a-mor,
voi kɛ sɑ-pe-tɛ kɛ k̲ɔ̲-sɑɛ ɑ-m̲o̲r̲,

don-ne ve-de-te, s'io l'ho nel cor,
d̲ɔ̲nːɛ ve-d̲e̲-tɛ siːɔ lɔ nel kɔr,

don-ne ve-de-te, s'io l'ho nel cor.
d̲ɔ̲nːɛ ve-d̲e̲-tɛ siːɔ lɔ nel kɔr.

Quel-lo ch'io pro-vo, vi ri-di-rò,
k̲w̲e̲lːɔ kiːɔ p̲r̲ɔ̲-vɔ, vi ri-di-r̲ɔ̲,

è per me nuo-vo, ca-pir nol so.
ɛ per me n̲w̲ɔ̲-vɔ kɑ-p̲i̲r̲ nol sɔ.

Sen-to‿un af-fet-to pien di de-sir,
s̲ɛ̲n-tɔun ɑf-f̲ɛ̲tːɔ pjɛn di de-z̲i̲r̲,

ch'o-ra è di-let-to, ch'o-ra‿è mar-tir.
k̲o̲-rɑ ɛ di-l̲ɛ̲tːɔ k̲o̲-rɑɛ mɑr-t̲i̲r̲.

Ge-lo,‿e poi sen-to l'al-ma‿av-vam-par,
d̲ʒe̲-lɔe pɔi s̲ɛ̲n-tɔ lɑl-mɑv-vɑm-pɑr,

e‿in un mo-men-to tor-no‿a ge-lar.
ein un mo-m̲e̲n̲-tɔ t̲o̲r̲-nɔɑ dʒe-l̲ɑ̲r̲.

Ri-cer-co‿un be-ne fuo-ri di me,
ri-tʃɛr-koun b̲ɛ̲-nɛ f̲w̲ɔ̲-ri di me,

non so chi'l tie-ne, non so cos'‿è.
nɔn sɔ kil t̲jɛ̲-nɛ nɔn sɔ kɔ-z̲ɛ̲.

So-spi-ro‿e ge-mo sen-za vo-ler,
so-spi-r̲ɔ̲e d̲ʒe̲-mɔ s̲ɛ̲n-tsɑ vo-l̲ɛ̲r̲,

pal-pi-to‿e tre-mo sen-za sa-per.
pɑl-pi-t̲ɔ̲e t̲r̲e̲-mɔ s̲ɛ̲n-tsɑ sɑ-p̲e̲r̲,

Non tro-vo pa-ce no-te, nè di, ma pur mi pia-ce lan-guir co-sì.
nɔn t̲r̲ɔ̲-vɔ pɑ-tʃɛ n̲ɔ̲tːɛ ne di, mɑ pur mi p̲jɑ̲-tʃe lɑn-g̲w̲i̲r̲ ko-z̲i̲.

Voi che sa-pe-te che co-sa‿è a-mor,…
ʋoi kɛ sɑ-pe-tɛ kɛ k̲ɔ̲-sɑɛ ɑ-m̲o̲r̲,…

Footnotes to Italian Pronunciation

- In multiple syllable words, the syllables that should be stressed are underlined.

- [ɾ] should be flipped.

- [r] should be trilled.

- Certain double consonants can be sustained on a pitch while maintaining a legato line, such as those in the words "donne" and "quello." The singer should take time for the singable double consonants in each of these words from the preceding musical note.

- There are other double consonants, such as those in the words "affetto" and "diletto," which interrupt the legato line when pronounced correctly. For example, when singing the word "affetto" [ɑfːfɛt-tɔ], the singer should briefly stop on the first [t], creating a slight silence before the sounding of the second [t].

TRANSLATION

You, who know what love is,
Ladies, see if I have it in my heart.
That which I feel, I will explain to you;
It is new to me; I don't understand it.
I sense an affection full of desire,
Which now is pleasure, now is agony.
I freeze, and then I feel my soul burning,
And in a moment I return to freezing.
I look for something beautiful outside of myself,
I don't know who holds it, I don't know what it is.
I sigh and moan without wanting to,
I quiver and tremble without knowing it.
I find no peace night or day
but yet it pleases me to suffer this way!
You, who know what love is,…

13. Voi che sapete

(You Know What Love Is)

Italian words by
LORENZO DE PONTE (1749-1838)
English words by **PATRICK M. LIEBERGEN**

from LE NOZZE DI FIGARO
Music by **WOLFGANG AMADEUS MOZART** (1756-1791)
Edited and Arranged by **PATRICK M. LIEBERGEN**

don - ne ve - de - te,____ s'io l'ho nel____ cor.
give____ me your an - swer,____ then I'll____ de - part.

Quel - lo ch'io pro - vo, vi____ ri - di - rò,____
Let me now tell____ you, all____ that I feel,____

è per me nuo - vo, ca - pir nol so.
it's ver - y new to me, is____ this love real?

Sen - to un af - fet - to pien di de - sir,____
I am so hap - py, full of de - sire,____

ch'o - ra è di - let - to, ch'o - ra è mar -
it gives me great plea - sure, pain, hot as

tir. Ge - lo, e poi sen - to l'al - ma av - vam -
fire. Fro - zen, my soul, then burn - ing like

par, e in un mo - men - to tor - no a ge -
flame, turns in a mo - ment cold at one

lar. Ri - cer - co un be - ne fuo - ri di me,
name. I seek a bless - ing that's not in me,

Where'er You Walk

George Frideric Handel (1685–1759)

George Frideric Handel was a renowned composer of instrumental and vocal works at the end of the Baroque era. Born in Halle, Germany, he took music lessons with Friedrich Wilhelm Zachau, and served as assistant organist at Halle Cathedral before moving to Hamburg to pursue his musical career. While in Hamburg he became a violinist in the opera house orchestra and composed his first opera, *Almira*. Handel then visited Italy in 1706 to learn the Italian style of composition, completing a number of successful operas as well as cantatas and instrumental music. After additional international travel, he eventually settled in England to become a leading musical figure as a composer of operas and oratorios, although he wrote a number of beloved instrumental pieces, such as *Water Music*, and ceremonial church music.

Handel became tremendously successful in England from the very beginning of his musical endeavors there. *Rinaldo*, his first opera for the people of London, was hailed as a great success, and subsequent works when he was a young man in his twenties brought him tremendous fame. Eventually becoming a leading figure in London's musical life, Handel was honored by both Queen Anne and King George I with financial backing and honors for his musical successes. His large-scale oratorios in English, including many exuberant choruses for the people, made him especially popular in England. Over 3,000 persons attended Handel's funeral in Westminster Abbey.

"Where'er You Walk" is from Handel's *Semele*. *Semele* was composed by Handel as a secular presentation meant to be presented on stage by soloists and a chorus without dramatic action. The libretto of *Semele* was the work of the esteemed British dramatist William Congreve, who originally called his work "an opera" when it was first published in 1707. However, its lack of dramatic qualities resulted in no composer using it until Handel decided to compose music based on a revision of Congreve's original work. Beginning the piece on June 3, 1743, Handel completed it in merely one month for presentation in the manner of an oratorio. Its premiere was quite unsuccessful to a large crowd on February 10, 1744 at the oratorio festival at Covent Garden. Although Handel subsequently reworked the score in an effort to improve the work, it never gained popularity and was never revived in Handel's lifetime.

The story of *Semele* is mythological and is a very involved story of the love relationships of many characters. Handel enjoyed setting the music in the spirit of the content, based on the theme of love. Although the work was unsuccessful for Handel and is rarely performed today, the music contains moments of great beauty. One memorable melody is that of "Where'er You Walk," an aria sung by Jupiter, a tenor soloist, in the Second Act. This melody is masterfully woven together between the solo and instrumental parts in Handel's setting.

Handel originally scored this solo with an accompaniment of first and second violins, viola and continuo in the key of B-flat major. This edition provides a keyboard part based on the original instrumental parts. Tempo and dynamic indications are further additions to Handel's original score.

14. Where'er You Walk

Words by
WILLIAM CONGREVE (1670-1729)

from SEMELE
Music by **GEORGE FRIDERIC HANDEL** (1685-1759)
Edited by **PATRICK M. LIEBERGEN**

Wher - e'er you walk, cool gales shall fan the glade; trees, where you sit, shall crowd in - to a shade, trees, where you sit, shall crowd in -

to_____ a shade.

Wher - e'er you walk, cool gales shall fan the__ glade;

trees, where you sit, shall crowd in - to a__ shade,_____

trees,   where— you— sit,

shall crowd———— in - to———— a shade.

Fine

rit. 2nd time

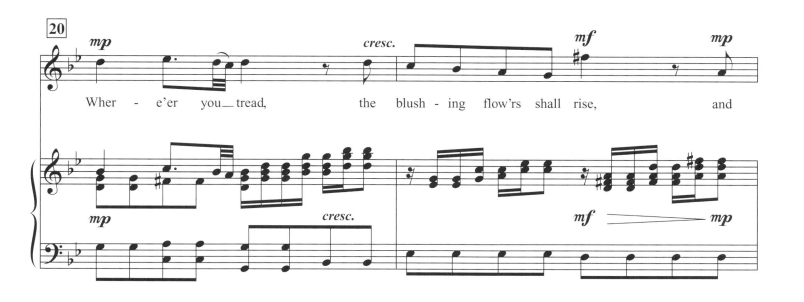

Wher - e'er you_ tread, the blush - ing flow'rs shall rise, and

all things flour - ish, and all things flour - ish wher -

e'er you turn your eyes, wher - e'er you turn your eyes, wher - e'er you turn your eyes.

You Raise Me Up

Rolf Løvland (1955–   )

"You Raise Me Up" was composed by Rolf Løvland, a very successful and internationally regarded Norwegian composer. Born in Kristiansand, in southern Norway, he formed his first band at the early age of nine before studying music at the Music Conservatory in Kristiansand and receiving his Masters degree in music at the Norwegian Institute of Music in Oslo. He then became one of Norway's most successful popular songwriters, earning a Norwegian Grammy Award and completing more than sixty national hits. He was also a two-time winner of the international Eurovision Song Contest in 1985 and 1995, and a four-time winner of Norway's Eurovision Song Contest.

Together with the Irish violinist Fionuala Sherry, he formed the group Secret Garden, combining a mixture of Nordic, Celtic and New Age music and sounds. Their debut album in 1996, *Songs From A Secret Garden*, became an immediate best-seller in Norway and internationally. Subsequent albums provided Løvland the freedom to explore a wide musical landscape of sounds.

Løvland, the group's composer, producer and keyboardist, originally wrote "You Raise Me Up" as an instrumental piece and titled it "Silent Story." The melody is based on fragments of the traditional Irish tune "Londonderry Air," which is best known as the melody of the 1910 song "Danny Boy." Løvland eventually approached Irish novelist and songwriter Brendan Graham to write words to the song. Graham's books *The Whitest Flower* and *The Element of Fire*, his two best-selling novels, had inspired both Rolf Løvland and Fionuala Sherry. Brendan immediately heard a story upon hearing the melody and proceeded to write lyrics titled "You Raise Me Up," drawing inspiration from his first book, *The Whitest Flower*.

Originally released on the 2001 Secret Garden album, *Once in a Red Moon*, with the vocals sung by Irish singer Brian Kennedy, "You Raise Me Up" quickly became popular in both Ireland and Norway. Also recorded by Daniel O'Donnell in 2003, his recording became well known throughout Ireland and the United Kingdom.

In 2003, Josh Groban was chosen by David Foster to record it, establishing Groban's career and the tremendous popularity of the song in the United States and internationally. Groban's recording was nominated for a 2005 Grammy award, and he sang it in many high profile events, including his appearances at Super Bowl XXXVIII, in a special NASA commemoration for the crew of the Space Shuttle Columbia disaster and with the African Children's Choir on television shows. Heard in numerous versions throughout the world, the song was nominated for the Gospel Music Awards four times, including "Song of the Year." Additionally, the version by the Christian group Selah went to No. 1 on Billboard's Christian Charts.

The arrangement provided here is in the spirit of the original release, with the violin slowly sounding the melody reminiscent of an Irish air. This inspirational gem should be fully expressed in performance with careful attention to word rhythms, phrasing and dynamics.

15. You Raise Me Up

with optional violin*

Words and Music by **ROLF LØVLAND**
and **BRENDAN GRAHAM**
Arranged by **PATRICK M. LIEBERGEN**

NOTE: *Begin at measure 8 for performance by voice and keyboard only.*

* Violin part is on pages 117–118.

When I am down and oh, my soul so wea-ry, _____ when trou-bles come and my heart bur-dened be, then I am still _____ and wait here in the si - lence un-til you come and sit a while _____ with

me. You raise me up so I can stand on moun - tains. You raise me up to walk on storm - y seas. I am strong when I am on your

You raise me
up so I can stand on moun - tains. You raise me

shoul - ders. You raise me up to more than I can

be. You raise me up to

more than I can be.

VIOLIN or OBOE

1. Domine Deus
(Lord, God Forever)

English words by
PATRICK M. LIEBERGEN

from GLORIA
Music by
ANTONIO VIVALDI (1678-1741)
Edited by **PATRICK M. LIEBERGEN**

CELLO

1. Domine Deus

(Lord, God Forever)

English words by
PATRICK M. LIEBERGEN

from GLORIA
Music by
ANTONIO VIVALDI (1678-1741)
Edited by **PATRICK M. LIEBERGEN**

FLUTES I & II*

10. Sheep May Safely Graze
(Schafe können sicher weiden)

German words by
SALOMO FRANCK (1659–1725)
English words by **KATHERINE K. DAVIS** (1892–1980)

from WAS MIR BEHAGT, IST NUR DIE MUNTRE JAGD
Music by **JOHANN SEBASTIAN BACH** (1685-1750)
Edited and Arranged by **PATRICK M. LIEBERGEN**

*or two C–Instruments

15. You Raise Me Up

Words and Music by **ROLF LØVLAND**
and **BRENDAN GRAHAM**
Arranged by **PATRICK M. LIEBERGEN**

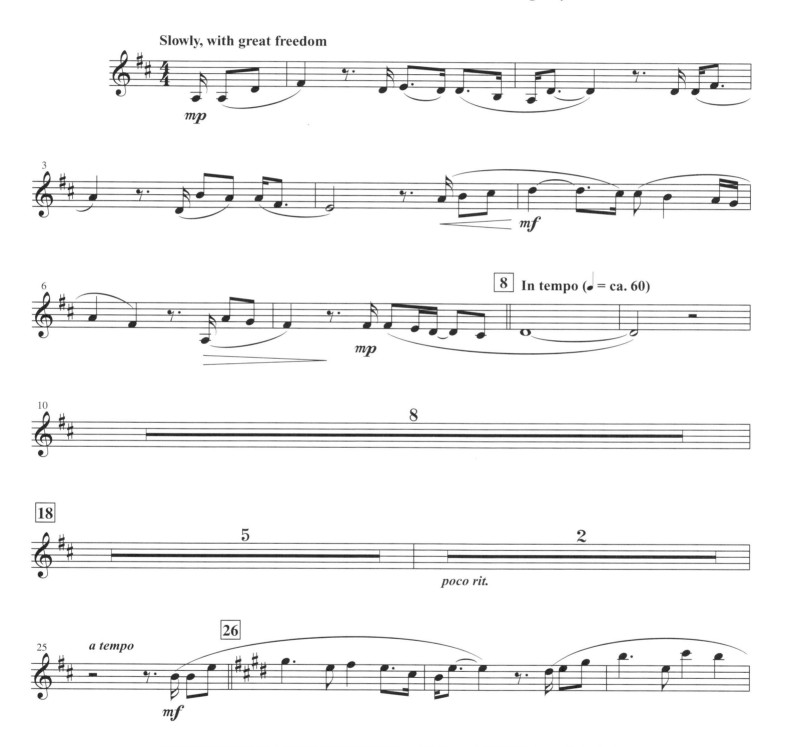

International Phonetic Alphabet Pronunciation Guide

IPA symbols used in this book with equivalent sounds in English:

Vowels

[a]	(first part of) light [laɪt], shout [ʃaʊt]
[ɑ]	dark, balm, father
[e]	came, make, gave
[ɛ]	let, many, friend
[ə]	lemon, even, oven
[i]	see, machine, receive
[ɪ]	sit, busy, gym
[o]	obey, bode, cloak
[ɔ]	shore, caught, raw
[ʊ]	book, look, good
[u]	you, who, tooth

Semivowels

[j]	yes, onion, you
[w]	was, sweet, suede

Dipthong:

[ɑɪ]	cry, night, pie

Consonants

[b]	baby, bat, bubble
[d]	dog, bed, do
[f]	life, fire, if
[g]	go, cigar, twig
[dʒ]	joy, jet, generous
[h]	house, who, hit
[k]	cat, tackle, choir
[ks]	ax, extreme, hexagon
[l]	alto, alleluia, let
[m]	hymn, mother, hum
[n]	pan, snail, nose
[p]	put, supper, sap
[s]	step, spin, course
[ʃ]	shoot, push, shine
[t]	hit, battle, tube
[tʃ]	cello, hitch, cheer
[v]	very, nerve, visit
[z]	nose, zebra, zoo

Additional IPA Symbols Used In This Book:

[ː]	Indicates to lengthen the previous vowel or consonant.

Vowels

[œ]	tongue position for [ɛ] and lip position for [ɔ], as in the German word "können" [kœ-nən].
[y]	tongue position for [i] and lip position for [u], as in the German word "glücklich" [glyk-lɪç].

Consonants

[ç]	Indicates that the tongue should be placed close to the palate in the position for the vowel [i] while at the same time sharply blowing air through that opening. Known as the "ich" sound, it closely resembles the initial aspirate sound in the English word "hue" that is emphasized.
[ɲ]	Indicates that the tip of the tongue should be in contact with the lower front teeth while the front of the tongue is raised and pressed against the front of the hard palate. Nasality is then produced when breath passes through the nose, as in the Italian word "sogno" [so-ɲɔ].
[x]	Indicates that an aspirant, voiceless sound should be produced by blowing air to cause friction between the soft palate and the back of the tongue, which is moved up toward the soft palate, as in the German word "wacht" [vaxt].
[ɾ]	a singular, flipped "r."
[r]	a trilled "r."
[ʎ]	Indicates a similar sound to [lj] in the word "million" [mɪ-ljən], requiring only one tongue action, as in the Italian word "voglio" [vɔ-ʎɔ].

Sources

Bach, Johann Sebastian. "Sheep May Safely Graze." *Was mir behagt, ist nur die muntre Jagd. Johann Sebastian Bachs Werke*. Ed. Bach-Gesellschaft. Vol. 29. Leipzig: Breitkopf & Härtel, 1881. 26 vols.

Gershwin, George. "I Got Plenty O' Nuttin'." *Porgy and Bess*. New York: Gershwin Publishing Corporation/Chappell & Co., Inc., 1935.

Handel, George Frideric. "Ombra mai fù." *Serse. George Friedrich Händels Werke*. Ed. Friedrich Chrysander. Vol. 92. Leipzig: Breitkopf & Härtel, 1884. 96 vols.

Handel, George Frideric. "Where'er You Walk." *Semele. George Friedrich Händels Werke*. Ed. Friedrich Chrysander. Vol. 7. Leipzig: Breitkopf & Härtel, 1860. 96 vols.

Løvland, Rolf. "You Raise Me Up." Universal Music Publishing and Peermusic (Ireland), 2002.

Mendelssohn, Felix. "O Rest in the Lord." *Elijah. Werke*. Ser. 13. Leipzig: Breitkopf & Härtel, 1877. 19 sers.

Mozart, Wolfgang Amadeus. "Non siate ritrosi." *Così fan tutte. W.A. Mozart's Sämtliche Werke*, Ser. 5. Leipzig: Breitkopf & Härtel, 1876-1905. 24 sers.

Mozart, Wolfgang Amadeus. "Voi che sapete." *Le nozze di Figaro. W.A. Mozart's Sämtliche Werke*, Ser. 5. Leipzig: Breitkopf & Härtel, 1876-1905. 24 sers.

Peri, Jacopo. "Gioite al canto mio." *Euridice*. Florence: Giogio Marescotti, 1600.

Purcell, Henry. "I Attempt from Love's Sickness." *The Indian Queen*. Ed. E. J. Dent. Vol. 19. London: The Purcell Society, 1912. 32 vols.

Sartori, Francesco. "Time To Say Goodbye." Double Marpot Edizioni Musical and Insieme Edizioni Musicali S.R.L., 1997.